Y0-EMK-359

Pictures

Teacher's Choice Series

Patrice Faraclas
Vacaville, California

Illustrations by
Sherry X. Chen

Dominie Press, Inc.

The development of the *Teacher's Choice Series* was supported by the Reading Recovery project at California State University, San Bernardino. All authors' royalties from the sale of the *Teacher's Choice Series* will be used to support various Reading Recovery projects.

Publisher: Raymond Yuen
Series Editor: Stanley L. Swartz
Illustrator: Sherry X. Chen
Cover Designer: Steve Morris
Page Design: Pamela S. Pettigrew

Copyright © 1996 Dominie Press, Inc. All rights reserved. No part of this publication may be reproduced or transmitted in any form or by any means without permission in writing from the publisher. Reproduction of any part of this book, through photocopy, recording, or any electronic or mechanical retrieval system, without the written permission of the publisher is an infringement of the copyright law.

Published by:

Dominie Press, Inc.
1949 Kellogg Avenue
Carlsbad, California 92008 USA

ISBN 1-56270-549-0
Printed in Singapore by PH Productions.
2 3 4 5 6 PH 99 98 97

I love to draw pictures.

I drew a picture for Mom.

She put it on the refrigerator.

I drew a picture for my teacher.
She put it on the wall.

I drew a picture for my friend.
She put it in her room.

I drew a picture for my sister.
She put it on her door.

I drew a picture for my grandma.
She put it in a frame.

I love to draw lots of pictures.

About the Author

Patrice Faraclas has a Reading Specialist Credential and a Masters Degree. She has been involved in education for 23 years and currently teaches at Sierra Vista Elementary School where she works as the Reading Specialist and Reading Recovery™ teacher. She lives in Vacaville, California with her husband, Makel, and her children, Nicole and Matthew.